A Journey Through My Soul

A Journey Through My Soul

On the Narrow Way

Michelle Elizabeth Rogers

2006

A Journey Through My Soul

THANK YOU

I want to thank my Father in Heaven for all the blessings in my life. He is the air I breathe and He is all the good in me. Thank you God for my family and friends that have supported and loved me, thank you for this amazing gift you given me. I hope that these poems will be a testament to You and a blessing to those that read them. And I want to thank Jesus for the precious gift of His blood. Thank you for that one-drop that cleanses me over and over again. Thank you for teaching me Your ways and guiding my steps along the path. Thank you Holy Spirit for your comforts, intercessions and bringing me truth and revelation of God's Holy Word.

Thank you my Father, my Savior and my Comforter!

A SPECIAL THANKS TO:

Traci Lee Marra – thank you for your support, love, and generosity. You have also been a significant part in my spiritual growth. Thank you for encouraging my walk and taking the journey with me!

Elizabeth Rogers – thank you Mommy for teaching me morals and for making each holiday and birthday special. You helped make my childhood happy and special.

David Rogers – thank you Daddy for all the times you drove us to Sunday school. Those times laid an important foundation in my life.

Candy Griffith – thank you to my Sister for the found memories we've shared as children. I still look back on so many of those memories and they make me smile. A little toe-head following me around, someone I tickled, punched in the arm and played rummy with.

Elizabeth & Paul Hanna – thank you for the holiday memories of fun, laughter and family togetherness. Those memories are cherished!

Lori Szymonowicz – thank you for giving me the title to this book, it is a perfect fit. And thank you for being a caring friend.

Juanita Taylor – thank you for the excitement and admiration you showed and encouraging me to publish this book of poetry.

Elisa Stowell – thank you for encouraging me to continue to write by telling me that I had raw talent, that compliment was the catalyst that kick-started my writing fervor.

Kathy Troccoli, Joyce Meyer, and Jennifer Knapp – thank you for sharing with me your gifts from God and making a difference in my life through the your anointing from God.

IN MEMORY OF...

I want to thank God for the people that he puts in my life. I have had some sad losses in my life that has made me realize how special my family and friends are to me. It isn't every day that someone is so blessed with so much love. I never want to take for granted the people that I love, because in an instance they can be gone.

Margaret Marra (Peggy) —my life is better for having known you, the example you displayed daily of kindness, generosity, upbeat and love has touched my life. You became a friend that I admired for your strength and love of your family. You are missed so very much!

Betty Lou Rodgers (Woo) — an amazing person that I was so fortunate to get to know. God blessed me with two wonderful years of Craft Shows with you, I'm so thankful for that time. You became a great friend that I admired and loved. Thank you for the fun and laughter we shared. I smile each time I think of you. I miss you Woo!

Two of the best dogs in the world:

Mikey (Biggie Boo) and Peppy (Misses) – I miss my doggies so much, you left too soon! But I am so very thankful for all the time I did get to spend with you, you both gave so much love and joy; I will miss you always. You were very special and sweet doggies. Mama's babies!

Dedicated to:

Ruth Elizabeth Hawkins

Thank you for all that you've done for me and all that you are to me. I thank God for your love, encouragement and support. And thank you for whispering the Name of Jesus in my ear when I was just a baby, for facilitating my walk with God and for being my biggest fan. I Love You!

He will straighten my crooked feet...

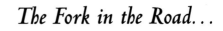

The Fork in the Road...

LEAD ME

Lead me dear Lord, for I fear I have lost my way
I have forgotten what is important; I have forgotten how to pray.
I feel so distant and I feel so alone
I need your guidance, to guide me home.
Please Lord hear my cry,
Hear my pleas and hear my sighs.
Sometimes I feel trapped in this shell
Wanting to fly away from this haunting hell.
I want the goodness to stay in my heart
These feelings of joy, please do not let them part.
This world is wicked and it bleeds my soul
Trying to take it over and make me cold.
So lead me dear Lord, lead me to the righteous path
Pull me up from the sludge and away from the wrath.
Please dear Lord, keep me in Your precious sight
Help me to know the difference between wrong and right.
Because I so desire to be better than I am,
To better this world and to better man.
That battle may always be losing, but at least I can try
Knowing I made a difference, even after I die.
And may my eyes be open to see
That each day, You are leading me.

Proverbs 3:5,6

Trust in the Lord with all thine heart; and lean not to thine own understanding. In all the ways acknowledge Him and He shall direct your paths.

My words,

As a human being I can tend to get off track easily and frequently. My walk with God is a constant prayer for guidance and to be led by the Holy Spirit. Even then I can get off track or not want to travel the road God has brought me to. It has been a struggle and a sacrifice to follow His lead at times. But I think that is the plan; it shouldn't be easy, otherwise everyone would do it. As a child of God there is a special task; to clear the rocks along the way, to battle the elements, to be protected from the avalanches, but most importantly to climb the mountain. In Genesis 22:14 the verse states "On the mountain of the Lord it will be provided." Not circling and not half way up, but to persevere to the top. The only way to do that I have found is through Jesus Christ! He will lead my steps and make straight the paths. He will always precede and follow me through the days of my life. It may be a struggle to continue on the path, but the prize at the end will be more than worth it.

Michelle Elizabeth Rogers

HAVE I BEEN FORGOTTEN?

Have I been forgotten, has He turned His face away
Is it because of the times when I was astray?
I pray each day that Jesus would hold me near
To ease my suffering and take away my fear.
Sometimes I feel so lost and I need His help
But I am afraid my soul has been shelved.
I want so much to feel His presence again
To feel His touch to make my heart mend.
I need to hear Him talk to me again
Because He is my best friend.
Without Him I know I would surely be lost
Because He has kept my heart warm to melt away the frost.
I will never leave my faith, because I want Him to know
That I love Him so much even though it is hard to show.
So please don't forget me Jesus, I need You in my life
I need You in the morning and I need You at night.
You are the best part of me; You made me what I am
The kind and loving person that I know I am.
So have I been forgotten, well I don't think so
Because I know He hears me, that I just know.
And if I ever feel lonely again
Then I will pray to talk with my friend.
Because there are so many that need Him more
So it is ok if my prayers He stores,
Just for the day when His time is free
And when He wants to just talk with me.

Psalm 69:13-14

But as for me, my prayer is to You, O Lord. At an acceptable and opportune time, O God, in the multitude of Your mercy and the abundance of Your loving-kindness hear me, and in the truth and faithfulness of Your salvation answer me. Rescue me out of the mire, and let me not sink; let me be delivered from those who hate me and from out of the deep waters.

My words,

There have been times when I felt my prayers went unanswered or stuck in a tree or something. But that won't stop me from continuing to pray. I have been blown away by the blatant answers that I have received to my prayers. I often times ask for God to speak clearly and loudly to me, because I don't get hints or subtleties. Then the next day or two, maybe three; something is done or said that is a direct answer to my prayer. Blows me away every time! Jesus said in John 15:7 "If you remain in me and my words remain in you, ask whatever you wish, and it will be given you." Prayer is an awesome thing!

Michelle Elizabeth Rogers

THE OPEN ROAD

The open road engulfs my soul; but still, I travel.
This trail of misery haunts me as my feet crush the gravel.
The vastness blinds me, never to reach the end
But still I move on, reaching a river bend.
I watch in silence at the life that goes on around me,
My eyes are so clouded, I can barely see.
There is nothing to see here, just tragedy and trash,
Another hopeless world, just waiting to crash.
I have seen it all in my existence, traveling on this open road
Carrying all that the world gave has been such a heavy load.
I don't worry much about the future that is waiting at my door
I just wonder about the consequence that life will lead me to endure.
So I go on further, there is no other choice
And no matter how loud I scream, no one will hear my weary voice.
My heart is frozen in time, as I am alone in my journey
I cannot stop; my will won't let me.
The air is still; my ears begin to ring from lack of sound
I walk with my Faith, still hoping to be found.
I will leave this road with everything I have known,
Leaving someone else to travel this open road.

Psalm 143:9-11

Rescue me from my enemies, O Lord, for I hide myself in you. Teach me to do your will, for You are my God; may Your good Spirit lead me on level ground. For Your name's sake, O LORD, preserve my life; in Your righteousness, bring me out of trouble.

My words,

I need to forget my past, because it was washed away by the blood of Jesus. The devil will try and throw it in my face using my family or friends to do it. But I have to forget the past and press on toward the goal that God has set before me. I can only do this through Jesus! His strength to walk on, His mercy to forgive me and teach me to forgive, His love to fill me, and His understanding to tolerate my sinful ways.

Michelle Elizabeth Rogers

THE DARK HOLE

The dark hole tries to suck me in each day,
It is a daily struggle not to give in to its way.
At times I stood on the edge and looked down
Not sure what I was looking to see, but happiness wasn't found.
I fell in once or twice, when stripped from me was my hope
But I managed to climb back out because Jesus was my rope.
I know what it is like in there; I have seen it for myself.
It is cold and lonely, sadness all around, not knowing where to go for help.
His light was always there, guiding me back again
Not only is He my Lord and Savior, but He is also my friend.
His light lives within me; the hole is dark no more,
He filled it with His love when I opened my heart's door.
There are times when the world blows in like the clouds
Trying to block His light and pull me down.
I can only resist because He is so strong
He tells me what is right and what is wrong.
Although I don't always listen, but I try to do my best
Because in Him is where I can find true happiness, peace and rest.
Now since I gave Jesus the key to my heart and soul
No longer do I have inside of me, The Dark Hole.

Psalm 143:7-9

Answer me quickly, O LORD: my spirit fails. Do not hide your face from me or I will be like those who go down to the pit. Let the morning bring me word of Your unfailing love, for I have put my trust in You. Show me the way I should go, for to You I lift up my soul. Rescue me from my enemies, O LORD, for I hide myself in You.

Psalm 119:27-29

Let me understand the teaching of Your precepts; then I will meditate on Your wonders. My soul is weary with sorrow; strengthen me according to Your word. Keep me from deceitful ways; be gracious to me through Your law.

My words,

I have felt down, sad, lonely and depressed at times. It is a scary and alone feeling, but I was never alone in those feelings. Jesus was there and will always be there to help me through and to bring me out of them.

Michelle Elizabeth Rogers

THE WITHERED LEAVE

The withered leave falls slowly to the ground
Inside this brain, I do not hear a sound.
A new life has begun, a time of solitude and hibernation
The wind is chilled leaving me with an eerie sensation.
The smell in the air is an amber musk
Standing here I watch as it falls to a gentle dusk.
Many colors fill my eyes; the awesome beauty of nature is so unseen.
Trapped in its "for granted" state, a modern day lean.
A once bright and pungent specimen is now a brittle brown speck.
Watching as leaves lose the tall tree's respect.
Soon each herd will be an apparition of life
Till the season has fulfilled its harsh strike.
Then the white blankets fortify its famine
Bringing on a new season to battle within.
The withered leave is just a speck,
From one's life journey hiding the wreck.
But the season prevails and the battle is won
New life begins and feet begin to run.

Romans 12:2

Don't copy the behavior and customs of this world, but let God transform you into a new person by changing the way you think. Then you will know what God wants you to do, and you will know how good and pleasing and perfect His will really is.

My words,

Thank God for His continual mercy and forgiveness through His Son Jesus. I can count the times I have sinned or even back slid. A once "pungent specimen", how many times I have turned into the brittle speck. But Jesus is the living water, He will continue to bring me back to that vibrant green leaf. What a wonderful gift!

Michelle Elizabeth Rogers

THE TREE AND THE CHILD

A seedling is sprouted, the gentle twig appears
A conscious has prevailed; the awakened soul is here.
The stem is strong to hold its form in the wind
A heated breath distilled in the night's grin.
The leaves grow from an instilled desire
A joyous heart breathes its own fire.
The spreading of the limbs, forms its own grace
A hiding of wills to disguise its own face.
Digging down deep it spreads its veins
It finds a presence but must fight the pain.
The tree holds tight, taking its form
The other I have watched has become its own swarm.
The branches have filled the air; the leaves are billowing in the sky
Just as once it learned to never to follow their lies.
Aging everyday, the tree loses its limbs
Grown now, the life travels to a new place to begin.
Yet it all seems so simple, the child that once smiled
But all has changed around it, the life and the trials.
The tree has towered beyond its intention
The love overflowing, beyond its mention.
If the tree shall not constraint to their needs
Then why should I learn to live by their means?

Isaiah 6:3

Holy, Holy, Holy is the Lord Almighty; the whole earth is full of His glory.

I Corinthians 9:24

Know ye not that they which run in a race run all, but one receiveth the prize? So run, that ye may obtain.

My words,

Jesus is the all-consuming fire. I love to watch a fire burn in my fireplace, watch how the flames completely engulf the wood. Not one spot of the wood is exposed; all is under the flame. I want my heart to be under the flame of Jesus. Not one spot exposed, renewing me daily. The "instilled desire" is the call that I feel to deepen my faith and climb that mountain.

Michelle Elizabeth Rogers

IMMERSE MYSELF

I sit on the dock, with only a toe to touch the water
Afraid to jump in, afraid to go under.
So I sit here sweating in the blazing sun
Letting it dry out my skin, till the blisters come.
And yet I cannot decide, I wait and I ponder
Should I stay here to see what is up yonder?
But I already know what is there, for I have seen it all,
The way my life has been and my continuous fall.
I cannot seem to let go, no matter how hard I try
To leave it all behind for that path that leads to the sky.
I want so much to sink in, to immerse myself completely
Soaking my skin, drenching my hair, under the water so freely.
To know the love that comes with that faith
And to feel my heart fill with that eternal grace.
Why can't I just jump in without looking back
The courage to follow it blindly, why does my heart lack?
For the water is clean and pure, but still I stay,
Knowing that with just a dip, the dirt would wash away.
I pray Dear God, please help me in,
Pull me down into the water, wash away my sin.
I long to be washed clean from the soot of this land
I long to washed by Your mighty hand.
In the waters of life, may I sink down deep,
May my heart and my soul, you Dear Lord keep.

Psalm 51:10,12

Create in me a pure heart, O God and renew a steadfast spirit within me. Do not cast me from our presence or take Your Holy Spirit from me. Restore to me the joy of Your Salvation and grant me a willing spirit, to sustain me.

My words,

One of the biggest things I've struggled with in my life is the ability to just "let go and let God"; always afraid of what is on the other side or what I will be missing. I've been on the other side and seen, participated and lived the other side. I've walked the fence between the two for years, making sure to jump off on the side that looked the best. Like a friend that would make plans until something better came along or wouldn't commit to plans, just in case. Well that is what is being done to God when walking the fence. Always wanting Him at beck and call, but not being committed to Him. Now being the friend that won't make definite plans, "just in case". That is a not a nice realization, but a truthful one. I have prayed and will continue to pray that I will immerse myself, jump off on the right side and ask Him to build a stockade so that I cannot get back up on that fence. I want to love better, pray more, worship right and trust completely in God who saved me with the precious gift of His Son's blood.

Michelle Elizabeth Rogers

Just one drop has cleansed me...

Sin gets in the Way. . .

THE PLAINS

I can't see the tree any more through the plains
It is dry and dusty here, it never rains.
The ground is stiff and brittle, and my feet are bare
It hurts to walk, but no one cares.
The sun doesn't shine here, it is always dusk.
And I can't see when the wind stirs up the dust
I saw her standing here once, that is why I came
I felt comfort in her presence, but it hasn't been the same.
It was green here then, the sun shown so high,
Running as fast as I could, just to be nigh.
The closer I got, the further she seemed
It was though all of it was just a dream.
Happiness invaded me, sunk deep into my bones
But now that she is gone, all I am is alone.
The tears soaked my cheeks and happiness faded
My life became lost, empty and jaded.
But still I stand here on the plains
No trees around to guard my weary mane.
The dust has filled my nose making it hard to breathe
But still I stand here and still I believe.
So I will stand here until she returns,
Until the grass is green again and the lesson is learned.
And I hope it won't be too long, for my feet sting from the pain,
For the sun to come out again and bring back the rain.

I Peter I:5-7

Praise be to the God and Father of our Lord Jesus Christ! In his great mercy he has given us new birth into a living hope through the resurrection of Jesus Christ from the dead, and into an inheritance that can never perish, spoil or fade—kept in heaven for you, who through faith are shielded by God's power until the coming of the salvation that is ready to be revealed in the last time. In this you greatly rejoice, though now for a little while you may have had to suffer grief in all kinds of trials. These have come so that your faith—of greater worth than gold, which perishes even though refined by fire—may be proved genuine and may result in praise, glory and honor when Jesus Christ is revealed.

My words,

There are many underlying tones in this poem. It is one of my favorites. It explains the pain felt in the heart after someone is lost. It is not a depressing poem, but one of hope and perseverance. To quote a very dear friend "Don't give up!"

Michelle Elizabeth Rogers

THERE'S AN UNNATURAL SOUL IN THE GARDEN

There's an unnatural soul in the garden; I see it at night
It wanders the marsh, searching for the light.
The light has abandoned it; it went for a better creature
Someone that has no shame, someone that has no leisure.
There is a pain that surrounds its being
Something that I have in its eyes, seen
It cries at night, shedding no tears
But it laughs in spite not to show any fear.
Mostly by day, it is transparent, nothing showing but its eyes
Just smelling the flowers, thinking it is invisible, I know to be a lie.
I watch everyday hoping to see its cast
Waiting on its features and hoping it will last.
There is wonder that fills my brain
I try to think of what caused this spirit to lose its name.
When the moon is big and bright, it shines through its glass frame
And its glow fades each night the light passes its hollow mane.
I have watched and I have waited for the light to call it home
While each day and night I have watched it roam.
When will the light call its name, when will there be a pardon?
For the unnatural soul that is still in the garden.

I Corinthians 7:23

God purchased you at a high price. Don't be enslaved by the world.

My words,

So often I get caught up in my material goals, even to the point of obsession. Not only does that take the fun out of what I am doing, but also it fills me with selfish feelings. I don't like to be all about myself, but sometimes I am. I guess that is just human nature, something that I will always fight. But I strive to keep myself on the bottom of the list, thinking and doing for others first. I'm not a selfish person and I hate selfish feelings! I have to remember that when they come I need to pray for Jesus to humble me.

Michelle Elizabeth Rogers

THE BLUENESS

Suspended and weightless, not feeling it cover me
I fly through this universe with no breath I can see.
My hair falls limp and my skin fills with lines
But this playground has trapped me with its watery vines.
Treading to keep the oxygen in my mouth
My chest constricts; the pressure thins me out.
There is a glimmer of light over in the distance; it shines in my eyes
I make my way there and uncover its disguise.
Nothing is there, no shred of hope is found
Blueness has won, keeping me in the surround.
I try to fight with the strength from within
But there is no chance to overpower, as I sink down in.
The frolic has come to an insignificant end
And the time has come to no longer pretend.
As I break free from its drenching grip and walk away alone
Feeling tired and cold, I gaze upon my battle zone.
Blue diamond crystals cascading in the light,
Drawing me in to finish the fight.
But it is not my battle, for that has already been won
And it no longer can keep me for I belong to the Son.

Ephesians 6:11

Put on the whole armor of God, that ye may be able to stand against the wiles of the devil.

My words,

This poem has both a spiritual tone and a frolic undertone. When I wrote it I was describing a specific activity. However, as I was writing it, unknowingly brought forth a spiritual meaning. I will give you a couple of key words, "Treading" and "Weightless" See if you can decipher the frolic undertone.

Michelle Elizabeth Rogers

AS THE BUTTERFLY...

As the butterfly searches for a haven from the hot sun
I clutch my soul and realize my life has just begun.
My world was so much more complicated then
My vision of existence was so complex, but yet so thin.
As the butterfly shifts from tree to tree,
I notice my life is no longer free.
The tales of time jab through my spirit, breaking down my key.
As the butterfly stops briefly on a unstable, swaying limb
I remember this morning; my reflection was so grim.
Noticing the toll on my life that reality has taken,
Trying to justify my love that has always been forsaken.
As the butterfly rethinks the flight, while resting for a spell
I look back on the paths I have chosen, some in regret, never to tell.
This existence of time has fulfilled my many wishes,
Holding on to quantity, as one at a time, I turn the pages.
As the butterfly circles one last time, realizing the end
I smile gently calling the butterfly my friend.
Seeing all the joy in my life never to fade
As the butterfly descends, so does this life I have made.

Romans 6:6, 23

Our old sinful selves were crucified with Christ so that sin might lose its power in our lives. We are no longer slaves to sin! For the wages of sin is death, but the free gift of God is eternal life
Through Christ Jesus our Lord.

My words,

This poem has a spiritual undertone. When I wrote it I was just starting to deepen my spiritual journey through His call. Not that I heard Him call my name or anything like that. It is just something I yearned more for; His presence, His strength and His comfort.

Michelle Elizabeth Rogers

SHUNNED

Long ago there was a woman that was wronged in so many ways
She grew bitter and angry and let sin fill her days.
Looking to fill the empty aching hole with the gluttony of worldliness
No matter how hard she loved, it didn't fill her with happiness.
So she drowned in her own self pity, shame written on her face,
Wondering why she could never find a true and happy place.
For she had all the money that she could spend
And never without the company of men.
Her life always empty, cold and hollow her soul,
But the day Jesus found her, He made her whole.
She walked into the room with a tear soaked face
Hearing their whispers, she has no right in this place.
Overwhelmed with the stain of sin that caused so much pain
She trembled when she saw Him, riddled with guilt and shame.
She knelt at His feet, cleansing them with her tears
And just one touch from His hand, freed her from sin and fear.
She anointed Him with oil as her life and love to Him forever
He filled her with His love, to leave her would He never.
I like Mary walked in my sin,
But Jesus does not condemn, He always looks within.
Condemned and unworthy still labeled by the righteous
But I will always be accepted, forgiven and loved by Jesus.

2 Thessalonians 3:5

May the Lord direct your hearts into God's love and Christ's perseverance.

Job 12:13

With Him is wisdom and strength, counsel and understanding are His

My words,

I am a daily sinner. I have done things in my past I am ashamed of. I continue to sin in my present day living. And I will sin in the days to come, whether it is cursing, anger, gossip, vanity, or apathy. There is a continual battle that goes on inside of me. Like Paul said in the bible; "For what I do is not the good I want to do; no, the evil I do not want to do—this I keep on doing." I love what is right, but I don't always do what is right! Thank God for His Son Jesus and His mercy on me. Jesus knows I am imperfect and will mess up. But I am also one of His children and just like I wouldn't reject my children, He will not reject me.

Michelle Elizabeth Rogers

THE LESSON OF THE TREE

Why did God create trees,
Was it because of their beauty of leaves blowing in the breeze?
Shade provided on a hot summer day
All of these are true in their own way.
But I think we over look the lessons they display.
Trees were born with leaves so beautiful and green
Then sin came into the world and made them unclean.
They stand tall, spreading out in pride
Just to capture His light on each side.
Then one by one, their limbs are invaded
The leaves are exposed and eager to be jaded.
They slowly die from the minute they were born
Drying and withering from the sun's unforgiving scorn.
Relief comes as the rain pours down
Sending the dirt from the leaves, falling on the ground.
The rain comes each time the dirt appears
Washing it clean from sin and fears.
Then the sun pulls back and the heat is less
And the tree sighs in the presence of rest,
Its leaves dry up, they begin to fall
And the tree slowly dies in spite of it all.
But the death is not physical or nothing else
The tree is only dying to itself.
It sheds its leaves like flesh from a bone
Standing naked in the sky with nothing for the wind to blow.
But then the leaves come back as soon as the sun returns,
And the cycle begins again, the lesson learned.
That even in the sun's scorching hot rays,
The tree knows that the rain will come and wash the dirt away.
And when the tree decides to let the leaves fly
They will rot off its frame as if to die.
Take a lesson from the tree, then maybe you will know
How to walk in your faith and which path to follow.

Romans 8:17

And since we are His Children, we will share His treasures, for everything god gives to His Son, Christ, is ours too. But if we are to share His glory, we must also share His suffering.

Matthew 5:3

Blessed are the poor in spirit, for theirs is the kingdom of Heaven.

My words,

I have always wondered if nature is a hidden example to use. Jesus spoke and taught in parables, using examples and stories to help the masses understand or receive revelation of the message according to His purpose for their life. Well just look at the tree, its many moods and changes. Voluntarily giving away its leaves, dying to itself until new life flows through its sap. I never understood "dying to self", "poor in spirit", or "taking up one's cross". But through study and revelation, my interpretation of it is taking the focus off me, not being out for myself, not being selfish. This could mean a different thing to anyone else. But for me, I work on being those things. It is an on-going lesson, one I can only learn from Jesus.

Michelle Elizabeth Rogers

He is the well that I drink from...

Becoming Aware. . .

LEFT BEHIND

Dear Jesus, I pray, help me to get by
Help me to know and understand the reasons why,
They left so suddenly, without warning or a clue
So now in my grief, I turn to You.
Please fill my heart with their warm memories and love
Please Dear Jesus, send me help from above.
I feel so afraid, so abandoned and alone
Not knowing where to turn or how to get home.
This hole in my heart bears nothing but pain
And the sorrow I feel is like cold, dark rain.
The memories of them can make me smile, if only for a moment
Still amazed how fast that precious time went.
They left me behind to follow a new road
And I am left here to carry this heavy load.
Maybe someday I can smile true again
Then the pain in my heart will begin to mend.
I miss them so much; it makes me want to scream aloud,
To say that it is not fair and I have been fouled.
But I will hold it in, maybe let out a tear or two
Shake my head in sorrow because there is nothing else to do.
They left me behind and life goes on,
Still so hard to believe that they are really gone.
So dear Jesus, please help me to stand again firm
Understanding the message that I have learned.
Looking to fill that hole in my heart, it is You I will find
And with You in my heart, I can deal with being left Behind.

Psalm 23

The LORD is my shepherd; I shall not be in want. He makes me lie down in green pastures, He leads me beside quiet waters, He restores my soul. He guides me in paths of righteousness for His name's sake. Even though I walk through the valley of the shadow of death, I will fear no evil, for You are with me; Your rod and Your staff, they comfort me. You prepare a table before me in the presence of my enemies. You anoint my head with oil; my cup overflows. Surely goodness and love will follow me all the days of my life, and I will dwell in the house of the LORD forever.

My words,

In my life I have been very blessed with family and many special people in my life. I thank God for them, praying for them always to be healthy and well. In 2000 I lost two very dear members of my family. Both in-laws, but still such a close and special part of my life. It was very hard to lose them and I still miss them both so very much. They added something special to my life! I thank God for memory! It is a gift that those who pass on will leave us with memories. And they can sustain us in our sorrow and grief that is life long. I can now smile and laugh when I remember the special times we've shared.

To Peg and Woo, we miss and love you still so very much!!!

Michelle Elizabeth Rogers

THROUGH THE EYES OF AN ANGEL

Sees the world as a loving place
Sees God's love in every human face,
Sees the children as reflections of Christ
Sees that every human soul has the ability to be nice.
Knows that sin will all be forgiven
Knows that life is worth living,
Knows that there is time to change
Knows that love could never be caged.
Feels that people are God's great creation
Feels the warmth from every nation,
Feels the love from the children's eyes
Feels God's grace come down from the sky.
Speaks of wonder and of the special gift
Speaks of the faith that will give a soul lift,
Speaks of Heaven and of its beautiful things
Speaks of the choirs of angels that sing.
Holds all life in the most cherished way
Holds God's words in what they say,
Holds each one of us in their eyes
Holds our lives and helps our cries.
Shows us what God has for us to know
Shows us all the love God has to show,
Shows us what rewards will come
Shows each day the morning sun.

Psalm 103:91-21

The LORD has established His throne in heaven and His kingdom rules over all. Praise the LORD, you His angels, you mighty ones who do His bidding, who obey His word. Praise the LORD, all His heavenly hosts, you His servants who do His will.

My words,

Angels are God's servants in Heaven and I am God's servant on earth. I only hope to be as good at my job as an angel is. In the prayer that Jesus gave us in the New Testament, the third line says "Thy kingdom come, Thy will be done, on earth as it is in Heaven". His will should be first in my life. This is an everyday struggle and God knows that, but I will continue that fight each day. Some days doing better than others. It certainly can't be done overnight, so I will continue my daily struggle and hope to overcome, even if a little at a time.

Michelle Elizabeth Rogers

DEAR MOM AND DAD

Dear Mom and Dad, I want you to know that I met Jesus today,
And I want you to know that I arrived here ok.
I am writing this letter from Heaven, where I now call my home
Jesus held me close to Him and said "My child, here is where you belong!"
This place is so wonderful; there is no sadness, no pain and no tears in
    sight
Just joy, happiness and eternal love from morning until night.
The day when I left you, my life on earth was complete
Even though it was so short, you must try not to weep.
I know that my time with you, went by so very fast
But please know that God called me home, for His special task.
I know you are still very sad, so do not be afraid to cry.
But I want you to know that here I have wings, and now I can fly!
You could never imagine all the beautiful things I now can see
And now my heart can open, because I am truly free.
Please feel secure to know that I am always beside you,
Each day and each night I will be there to watch over you too.
You have so much left to do so you must try somehow to go on,
God has such a big plan and He needs you to be strong!
You could never understand, so you must trust me on this
And someday soon we will meet again and share eternal bliss.
Because there was so much love and happiness you gave to me
I will always cherish and treasure my time with my family.
So take each day as a step into the future
But do not dismay, for I will always be with you.
And each step that you take, remember, I will not be far away
Because your love is still with me every day!
And until the day when I will again see your face
I will always remember that one special place,
Where I was a child and loved with everything I had
And called to you both, Dear Mom and Dad.

Revelation 21:3-5

And I heard a loud voice from the throne saying, "Now the dwelling of God is with men, and he will live with them. They will be his people, and God himself will be with them and be their God. He will wipe every tear from their eyes. There will be no more death or mourning or crying or pain, for the old order of things has passed away." He who was seated on the throne said, "I am making everything new!" Then he said, "Write this down, for these words are trustworthy and true."

My words,

I wrote this poem for someone that had a friend that lost a child. I can't say that I understand what someone goes through that has lost a child. Nor would I want too, but I can empathize with the sorrow and pain of losing someone that is a part of you. It doesn't seem fair that children should be terminally sick, abused or die too soon. As a child, I wished away years to become a grownup. Now that I am that grownup, I miss the days of my childhood. But those kids who are stricken with illnesses don't wish away the years, but savor everyday they can smile and love with their family. Time is precious, people are precious! Cherish that special person(s) in your life, taking time and making time, before you wish for more time.

Michelle Elizabeth Rogers

ANGELS

There is a spiritual realm that lay at my feet
I have read about it and heard about it, now I choose to seek.
Those that are invisible and surround me
Why are my eyes so blind to see?
I have walked many miles in my life, some so terrible to recall
I know there has been guidance, I felt it catch my fall.
But there are times when I feel so alone,
Trapped in silence, I still make my home.
I don't know the criteria of which I should keep,
Should I put it from my mind and hope someday I will meet?
Or should I take watch and aspire to find
Those beautiful winged apparitions that are not of our kind?
They say angels walk among us, do we meet them here and there,
In a world so wicked, why would they even care?
Still I believe that they are near, to watch over us and guide us through our
fright.
Some that stands guard while little ones sleep through the night.
So I hope someday, those I will see,
The angels that keep watch over me.

Psalm 91:9-12

If you make the Most High your dwelling, even the Lord, who is my refuge, then no harm will befall you, no disaster will come near your tent. For he will command his angels concerning you to guard you in all your ways; they will lift you up in their hands, so that you will not strike your foot against a stone.

My words,

I am not sure if I have ever seen an angel, but I have known and still know some wonderful people that are full of the Spirit of God. When praying for help, God dispatches angels to help in accordance to His own Will. Therefore, shouldn't it be taken seriously and into daily practice what Jesus said in John 13:34-35 "So now I am giving you a new commandment: Love each other just as I have loved you, you should love each other. Your love for one another will prove to the world that you are my disciples." If just by chance there is an angel (Heavenly or earthly) in my path, let me not be short, ignorant, rude or dismissive to them.

Michelle Elizabeth Rogers

BLACK SNOW

Pure and untouched, it falls from the sky
Just like the gentleness of a newborn's cry.
It glistens in the dark, providing its own light,
Lighting up the darkest of night.
It is perfect as it cascades on the ground
Not a footprint can be seen, no earth can be found.
The blanket lies down, protecting its very nature
Deep enough to keep away the evil creature.
But time is an enemy to this blanket of snow,
The sun slowly melts it and then the ground begins to show.
The cars that go by blacken it with each pass
Taking away its beauty, only the soot will last.
So many footprints now can be seen
Like scars in flesh, only they don't bleed.
As time passes the blanket grows thinner
And the snow gets blacker.
But then the snow falls down again one night
Building up the footprints and taking them out of sight.
Covering the black soot, now making it clean
No longer can any damage be seen.
The snow is new again; it begins a new fight
Hoping for the long and still of the quiet night.
This battle is endless; it is as oldest story I know
And nature will never stop the fight against the Black Snow.

Jeremiah 31:34

For I will forgive their wickedness and will remember their sins no more.

Isaiah 53:12

For He bore the sins of many, and made intercession for the transgressors.

My words,

How can something so pure turn so filthy? The progression of this world has turned beauty into a poisonous filth. There is so much out there that poisons a mind, soul and spirit. Turns them black like coal. Just looking at a newborn baby and then looking at myself, I am amazed at how things can turn. But with the continual cleansing flood of Jesus, I don't have to be soot covered. I am cleansed daily by His love, His mercy and His Blood.

Michelle Elizabeth Rogers

CHASING THE WIND

Did you ever stop and wonder what life really meant
About the useless blunder in a day that is spent?
The mindless thoughts of the world and its clutter
The energy drains that causes life to sputter.
Worry that takes a life away
And sinful retreats engaged in each day.
Focused on success that defines one's self
Still all the while placing the soul on a shelf.
A big house, fancy car, things that define worth
But that is human nature, instilled since birth.
It is all like chasing the wind,
Every materialistic thing.
Do you realize these things don't matter?
All they do is cloud the mind with clatter!
It is like chasing a wind that cannot be seen
A pointless, meaningless task it does seem.
A good life consists of the simpler things,
A happy and light heart that loves and sings.
Simple pleasures that don't clutter the mind
And a soul where God is easy to find.
Practical living that won't taint one's health
And the knowledge that love is greater than wealth.
Because the rules of this world will only destroy the soul
And chasing the wind will never make you whole.

Luke 12:15,34

Jesus said, "Beware! Don't be greedy for what you don't have. Real life is not measured by how much we own". Wherever your treasure is, there your heart and thoughts will also be.

Luke 16:13

"No one can serve two masters. For you will hate one and love the other, or be devoted to one and despise the other. You cannot serve both God and money."

My words,

In the book of Ecclesiastes, it talks a lot about "chasing the wind". Running after material possessions is pointless when considering that you can't take it with you. What is it going to matter how big a house is, or how much jewelry is locked up in a safe, or even how nice a car is? If material things are what fills the heart, then what is left for anyone else? Jesus said, "I have come so that you may have life and have it in abundance." He wants nice things for us and He blesses us with all that we have, but the heart should be filled with love because God is love and with God all things are possible!

Michelle Elizabeth Rogers

Open my eyes and my heart, O Lord...

The Awakening...

THORNS AND THISTLES

It is here they strangle me, these thorns and thistles
Weighted by the world and the sins that prickle.
Drowning in thoughts that only cause pain
Lead to another road soaked by torrential rain.
How can I win, where can I find the tools
Something that will free this eternal strangle hold?
But what when that is gone, there are rocks that will thwart
The goodness from digging down deep in mine heart.
I cry out, Oh Father!
Break up that dirt and scrape off the callus,
Don't leave me in this state of misery and malice.
I cannot do it alone, for thirty-nine years I have tried
Only to gain nothing, in vain I have cried.
So I am asking now, Oh God of my soul,
Please forgive me and loosen this garrote hold.
For only You have the tools that can achieve this task,
Unbound my heart from sin's evil grasp.
Splinter the rocks that impede love's growth
And make plentiful the seedlings of fruit in sooth.
Then in this testimony of my heart's blessed vary
I will not forget and I will not tarry,
But to keep the precepts of my Father's creed
Because it is He that plants the seed.

Mark 4:2-8

And He taught them many things in parables, and in His teaching He said to them: Give attention to this! Behold, a sower went out to sow. And as he was sowing, some seed fell along the path, and the birds came and ate it up. Other seed fell on ground full of rocks, where it had not much soil; and at once it sprang up, because it had no depth of soil; and when the sun came up, it was scorched, and because it had not taken root, it withered away. Other seed fell among thorn plants, and the thistles grew and pressed together and utterly choked and suffocated it, and it yielded no grain. And other seed fell into good soil and brought forth grain, growing up and increasing, and yielded up to thirty times as much, and sixty times as much, and even a hundred times as much as had been sown.

My words,

I wrote this poem in 2005 after an eye-opening sermon by my pastor. She told me that it is what is in the heart of a person that matters most. What the parable of the seed speaks to me is my heart and how God's word is absorbed. I want my heart to be good soil for each seed that lands to be rooted deep and spout forth fruit. With the pressures and busyness of the world it can turn a heart dry and brittle, filled with thorns and thistles strangling out God's Word. I found that when I lack in praying, in reading and in attending church a crust builds up on my heart. But He is faithful and awesome, renewing me, being patient with me and forgiving me over and over! What an incredible gift, "Mercy"!

Michelle Elizabeth Rogers

IF SOMEONE ASKED ME...

If someone ask me "Could you be without the rain
The warm summer rain, that comes down as the sun still shines.
The rainbow that appears and is never the same,
Would this cause you any pain?"
If someone asked me "Could you be without the trees
And the green leaves that sway gently in the breeze.
The shade they provides on a hot summer day,
Would this make you want to run away?"
If someone asked me "Could you be without Spring,
The beautiful flowers or the birds that sing
The songs that wake you so gently in the morn,
Would this make you want to be unborn?"
If someone asked me "Could you be without sunshine,
The warm soft rays that light the world all the time.
The colorful setting it always provides,
Would this make you want to hide?"
If someone asked me "Could you be without love
Something that fills your heart from above.
The very core that guides your being,
Would this make your heart stop beating?"
If someone asked me these questions, what would I say?
I could not be without any one of them, in any way.
For these are gifts and all of them are free,
Given by God for the entire world to see.
But if someone asked me, "Could you be without God,
Or faith that keeps your soul alive
Would this make you want to die?"
If someone asked me a question so absurd,
My answer would be, "Have you not heard?
I would be without all these things in the world,
But I could never be without the love of the Lord my God!"

I Corinthians 2:9

But, as it is written, eye hath not seen, nor ear heard, neither has entered into the heart of man, the things which God hath prepared for them that love Him.

I John 4:7

Let us love one another, for love comes from God. Everyone who loves has been born of God and knows God.

My words,

Since the day I can recall memories, Jesus has been a part of my life. I could never and would never want to be separated from Him. What a scary and alone place that would be. I have backslid a few times in my life, questioned Him, turned my back on Him and blamed Him. Still He stayed, always feeling His presence with me and receiving a constant flow of blessing and favor. I am regretful of those times and I still struggle with my own will and the constant battle between the flesh and the spirit. I thank God for His Holy Word, when it states in Romans 8:39 "neither height nor depth, nor anything else in all creation, will be able to separate us from the love of God that is in Christ Jesus our Lord."

Michelle Elizabeth Rogers

MY TEMPLE

My Temple cannot be encroached upon with a hollow purpose
For its depth goes beyond any surplus.
It contains my lifeline, my path and my way
It gathers love and it fills with joy day after day.
Overflowing with prayer on each day's end
Never for one day in vain should be spent.
It can not be heard, nor can it be seen
For I alone carry its key.
And it cannot be entered by any means
But it does contain my thoughts and dreams.
There are no floors or glass of any kind
For this temple I can only find.
There is not a day that goes by that I do not visit this place.
For it holds the image of God's beautiful face!
I have listened to the angels singing in this hall
I have cried and prayed for God to catch my fall.
The echoes of the Word always pass through
To give me hope and maybe a lesson or two.
And each day I listen and wait for the next
Hoping that God will return and I will be blessed.
I will never leave it; it shelters me from the cold
For you see My Temple is my Soul.

Psalm 27:4

One thing I ask of the LORD, this is what I seek: that I may dwell in the house of the LORD all the days of my life, to gaze upon the beauty of the LORD and to seek him in his temple.

My words,

Soul, spirit and mind; the most private places one can escape to. Dreams, imaginations, and fantasy can come to life within the mind. It can be a comforting place and a scary place; it can be a pure place and a filth pit. The lines are thin and easily crossed. What a temple should be filled with is love and hope always thinking of others. Easier said than done, I know I've been there and still am there. The gateway to all of these things is the eyes, what is taken in is what will fill the soul, spirit and mind. That is why there is a need to nourish them like to nourish the body. A body can't live on junk alone; it needs vitamins and oxygen. Call on the Holy Spirit, He will be sure to remove the muck that has been put in your life. Just like a hot shower after a sweaty afternoon in a garden feels great; how great it will feel to be cleansed by the Holy Spirit!

Michelle Elizabeth Rogers

A LETTER TO GOD

I wrote a letter to God today
Asking Him to lead me on my journey's way.
I don't know if I spoke it right
Or if I was even in His sight.
But I know He heard me when I say
"Oh Lord, Please hear me when I pray!"
I told Him about all the things I have done
And ask for forgiveness for every one.
I shed a tear to admit my shame
I said to Him, "Dear Lord, I am to blame!"
I ask him to help me and guide me to the right path.
I ask most of all to be more like Him, to avoid the final wrath.
But He did not judge me, nor did He turn away,
He listened to each and every word I had to say.
I told Him that I loved Him with all my heart
And gave Him my life, so we would never be apart.
I heard Him whisper so gently in my ear
"My child, never worry; for I am always near!"
I spoke again to pray for my family's good health,
But never in arrogance would I ask for fame, fortune or wealth.
And at the end of my letter, although I did not write it with a pen
All of my love to Him, that I would surely send.
Now each day for all of my life and forever more
I will write a letter to God, My Father and My Lord!

Psalm 86:5-7

You are forgiving and good, O Lord, abounding in love to all who call to You. Hear my prayer, O LORD; listen to my cry for mercy. In the day of my trouble I will call to You, for You will answer me.

Philippians 4:5-7

Let your gentleness be evident to all. The Lord is near. Do not be anxious about anything, but in everything, by prayer and petition, with thanksgiving, present your requests to God. And the peace of God, which transcends all understanding, will guard your hearts and your minds in Christ Jesus.

My words,

When I wrote this poem I was using the term "letter" as a symbol of my prayers. I used to think that prayers had to be beautifully spoken, long and filled with scripture. This is not the case; prayers can be spoken in the way I speak them. God is not expecting me to be a well-rehearsed evangelist. I believe what He wants is for me to include Him in every part of my life and my day, using prayer to speak to Him about my wants, needs, cares, worries, etc. throughout the day, everyday.

Michelle Elizabeth Rogers

MAY MY FAITH

May my Faith keep me on the right path
Please Dear Lord, hide me from thine wrath.
Keep me safe from all that is evil
And when I fall down, please let me heal.
May my Faith keep me close to God
May I always be worthy of His Love.
To keep the touch with His hand from above
And Dear Lord, may I always give just because.
May my Faith, I Pray, make a better person of me
May then my eyes will open so I will truly see,
And forever then will I always be
Part of Your Love and part of Thee.
May my faith lead me to His open arms
So I will be sheltered from all that is harm.
May I always be deserving of the attention I seek
And may I always be strong, but may I stay meek.
Dear Lord, may you help me to keep my faith strong
May you teach me so I know when I am wrong.
And shall I always be a lamb of your flock
So that my Faith will keep me upon You, my Rock.

Hebrews 11:1

Now faith is being sure of what we hope for and certain of what we do not see.

My words,

What is faith? Confidence, trust, reliance, assurance and conviction.
Confidence in saying that God is my creator and creator of all things.
Trust in God for all my issues.
Reliance on God that He will deliver me.
Assurance that He gave His Son, Jesus, to die for me.
Conviction in His word and abiding in Him.

Michelle Elizabeth Rogers

JUDGE

I cannot judge you, nor should you judge me
For what is in plain view, is not all you should see.
Jesus forgives; He has forgiven you too
So you should not judge the things that I do.
My heart is with God, as well is my Soul
Trying to find a place in this world that is not so cold.
Was it a law or a commandment, did I break
Or was it your beliefs, did I forsake.
It is my heart that is true and my faith that is strong
And it is God, not you that teaches me right from wrong.
Your glass house must be very secure
Casting your stones without ever shutting the door.
It is hypocrisy you live, if you think that you are just
Buried in your sin of lies, greed and lust.
For if you read His Word, then you will know what is true
That He is only my judge, it is never you.
So take your shallow thoughts and your judging heart away
Because I do not need your forgiveness to pray.
My faith is in the Word and God has spoken it all
And when I am to be judged, then He will call.
But till then; look upon yourself as you do me
It is not only your face in the mirror, but also your sin that you see.

Matthew 7:2-4

For in the same way you judge others, you will be judged, and with the measure you use, it will be measured to you. "Why do you look at the speck of sawdust in your brother's eye and pay no attention to the plank in your own eye? How can you say to your brother, 'Let me take the speck out of your eye,' when all the time there is a plank in your own eye?

My words,

I wrote this poem after an experience I had with a few Christians that laid judgement and condemnation on me. Those that are righteous in God are only righteous because of Jesus, not because of their own "good" works. These people are self-righteous, legalistic hypocrites that think they have the right to judge. In John 3:17 it states "God did not send His Son into the world to condemn it, but to save it." Christians should edify, not be critical or judgmental. God is the only judge! Sin is sin in His eyes; not one differs from the other. "People in glass houses shouldn't throw stones." What a great saying that is and fits so well! May I always consider my glass house before throwing stones.

Michelle Elizabeth Rogers

JESUS, MY ROCK

Each night I call upon my Rock
This gentle Lamb that has brought me to His flock.
We talk together like life long friends
So much hope and love to my heart He sends.
He taught me to lay my troubles down at His Feet
And He showed me that my soul, He shall always keep.
He taught me to believe in the Holy Word
And each promise He spoke opened my heart and I truly heard.
I know that He is with me each step that I take
And I know that His Love, I would never forsake.
My eyes are only filled with the beauty that is the Lord
And my ears are only filled with the sounds of His Holy Word.
He has given to me the greatest gift of all
He has given to me, the strength not to fall.
So He will hold my heart in His eternal Hands
No matter where I turn on the rocky land.
And now until forever my love I will always send
Never to falter, never to end.
I shall always follow the Lamb and the flock
And I will always call on Jesus, My Rock.

Psalm 118:14

The Lord is my strength and my song, and has become my salvation

II Samuel 22:2

The Lord is my rock, and fortress, and my deliver.

My words,

The wonderful words from Psalm 23, "The Lord is my Shepherd, I shall not want..." He is my rock, my foundation and my firm place. Without it, I would certainly fall. Jesus said in Matthew 24-27 "Therefore everyone who hears these words of mine and puts them into practice is like a wise man who built his house on the rock. The rain came down, the stream rose, and the winds blew and beat against that house; yet it did not fall, because it had its foundation on the rock. But everyone who hears these words of mine and does not put them into practice is like a foolish man who built his house on sand. The rain came down, the streams rose, and the winds blew and beat against that house, and it fell with a great crash." What is our "house"? My house is my heart, soul, and spirit. What is the "rain"? My rain is trials, temptations. I thank Him for being my rock and my shield against the storms in life.

Michelle Elizabeth Rogers

Through His Blood, I am a new creature...

Restoring My Soul. . .

THE GENTLE WAY

It is the gentle way I hear His whisper and it fills my soul.
I listen to His voice; it covers me from head to toe.
I heed His knowledge to learn all that I can
And open my heart so that I can reach His Holy Hand.
It is the gentle way I speak His words from my throat
They fall from my mind, the Holy words God wrote.
Sentences linger in the air with angels' voices behind it all
The music of the words that have been said, catch my fall.
It is the gentle way I can feel Him touch me, deep into my flesh
Warding off the damage caused by the wretch.
His fingers grip my soul, holding me tight
Keeping me warm, keeping me from fright.
It is the gentle way I can see His beauty radiate from above
Shining down and flying freely as a white dove.
The light covers my face to reveal His name,
A wonderful sight upon my weary mane.
It is the gentle way He gives me my life,
The way He guides me and keeps me through the night.
The glory of His own name restores my very soul
And unconditionally His love is there, always new, never old.
For God has touched me with his grace
For God has shown me his beautiful face.
For God has said to me, and I hear everything He has to say
For God has given to me The Gentle Way.

Luke 1:46-47

My soul glorifies the Lord and my spirit rejoices in God my Savior.

My words,

This was one of the very first Spiritual poems I wrote to God. I received a second calling several years ago. This calling brought me into a deeper relationship with God. I experienced the presence of the Holy Spirit in me. Revelations, wisdom, discernment, and unexplainable joy beamed inside of me. Still with so many barriers I held and still hold up, the Holy Spirit moved me. I often wonder if I could lay down these barriers that joy. That feeling from the Holy Spirit would probably be like a dam just broke overflowing in me. I still pray for God to bring these barriers down and blow them into smithereens, but I have to wait on Him for His time and receive the blessings in His order. What an amazing thing to be on, the blessings list of God!

Michelle Elizabeth Rogers

HUMBLE ME

I come to you Jesus; my spirit is broken in two
Only you know what my heart has been through.
I have been so wrong and let You down
And so many times I have fallen and hit the ground.
I think I am so strong at times
And I think I am invincible and can fly.
Humble me Abba; help me to pray when I am weak
Help me to find the path I so desperately seek.
Teach me how to deny myself each day
And forgive me when I do not want to pray.
Teach me how to give You my burdens, though many or few
Help me to always have faith and to trust in You.
For You are humble and gentle, Your burden is light
Please help in the battle when it is myself that I fight.
I cannot stand on my own; I would not want to try
And forgive me Holy Father, when I question You and ask why.
So humble me Jesus and show me Your way,
Teach me to call upon Your strength each day.
And if my anger begins to rage or my pride to show
Raise me up dear Lord, before I sink too low.
May Your glory always shine and fall upon me
As You teach me to be gentle and You humble me.

Proverbs 16:18-20

Pride goes before destruction and a haughty spirit before a fall. Better it is to be of a humble spirit with the meek and poor than to divide the spoil with the proud. He who deals wisely and heeds word and counsel shall find good, and whoever leans on, trusts in, and is confident in the Lord--happy, blessed, and fortunate is he.

Micah 6:8

He has showed you, O man, what is good. And what does the Lord require of you? To act justly and to love mercy and to walk humbly with your God.

My words,

Pride is one of the 7 deadly sins. I consider myself a meek person, but I'm sure there are some instances of arrogance in me. I am proud of certain accomplishments, but I am thankful that He has seen me through and has given me the gifts I have. In the Beatitudes, Jesus said, "Blessed are the meek, for they will inherit the earth." I want to be humble in all I do and say, think and feel. When I do show pride that it is in the confidence of my Lord. Like all things that are of this world, it is a battle, one that I cannot win. It is the battle only through the blood of my Savior can win.

Michelle Elizabeth Rogers

BLIND

God blessed me with sight so that I may see
All the beautiful things He created for me.
But what my sight has taken away,
Was my heart's ability to love in every way.
Taken for granted the beauty of the world,
Believing what is seen instead of the Holy Word.
Looking with judgement because of the hypocrite I am
Never really seeing the beauty within.
I have seen wickedness and it has clouded my sight
Weaving its blinders to make everything seem right.
Judgement and hate fill my eyes each day
With every person that crosses my way.
Oh dear Jesus, please make me blind
Make my eyes not see so my heart can find.
Find the beauty that goes deeper than skin,
Loving not from my eyes but from what is within.
Then maybe I will truly see
Not to judge on beauty, what race or color they may be.
And may my eyes be finally open to see
God's love and grace shining down on me.

John 9:39

Jesus said, "For judgment I have come into this world, so that the blind will see and those who see will become blind."

My words,

When I say "make me blind", it is a metaphor. What I mean is make my heart blind. I get caught up in the world with wealth, fame, and beauty being tossed around like it should be the most sought after thing. I don't want to have my feelings of someone hinge on their looks, wealth, clothes, righteousness, or neighborhood. Seeing people as He sees them and treating them the way He treats them is the thing I strive for. It is not easy and it is a struggle for me at times, but I will continue to pray about this and hope to treat people as good as I want them to treat me.

Michelle Elizabeth Rogers

MICHELLE ELIZABETH ROGERS

THE WIND OF PEACE

Through the mist of the trees,
I hear a voice as soft as a breeze.
It runs through my body like a train with great force
And with every breath I take, I feel the wind take its course.
Through the darkness of each night
I feel His presence to comfort my fright.
Though my fear is just an image of time
I still wait on Him to be shown a sign.
I may never know the secret of my living
But that will never stop my heart from giving.
For His presence has filled my soul with love
Touching my heart with His hand from above.
By hope and faith, I have bounded my life
Never to shun this bright and eternal Light.
I hold onto His Hallowed Name in all I say
And to honor Him always with all that I pray.
And with the wind that blows through my trees,
It will lead me to a place, modestly down on my knees.
The Wind of Peace will surround my spirit with love
A justification of my faith, the gentle breeze from above.

Psalm 95:6

Come, let us bow down in worship. Let us kneel before the Lord our Maker.

My words

It is futile to swim against the current in a river. Once it has control, it is easier to let it guide. The same is true once considered a child of God. I am no longer in charge of my footsteps. But still I resist at times and try to swim against the current, before finally tiring and giving Him my hand to guide me. I want to not resist, but to trust Him always. Knowing that when I do, I always come to realize that it was His way that was the best way.

Michelle Elizabeth Rogers

OUT THE WINDOW

There is a window between life and me, it doesn't open
The glass is sometimes frosted, sometimes clouded over.
I look out the window and imagine different lives in my mind
The one I dream is me, isn't the one I find.
But I can see me out there when I'm feeling strong
That strength only lasts for a moment and then it is gone.
So I am back to pounding on the glass, hoping someone will see
Praying for my Savior to rescue and set me free.
This window I have made keeps me alone
It protects me from the outside, so I don't roam.
But I get tired of breathing the same stale air
I want to be outside, feeling the wind in my hair.
And feel the drops of water when it begins to rain
But the window doesn't open; I can't break its thick pane.
I know someone that can and He is helping me now
To peel away each layer of the pane, Jesus is showing me how.
Now the glass isn't frosted, not clouded over anymore
Because those layers I've peeled away, now lay on the floor.
So I will continue to peel them away
With the help of my Savior each day.
Till one day the window will open with ease
And I will be able to feel life's precious breeze.
No longer afraid to learn and grow
Never to settle again for just looking Out the Window.

Romans 15:4-6

For everything that was written in the past was written to teach us, so that through endurance and the encouragement of the Scriptures we might have hope. May the God who gives endurance and encouragement give you a spirit of unity among yourselves as you follow Christ Jesus, so that with one heart and mouth you may glorify the God and Father of our Lord Jesus Christ.

My words

So many times throughout my life I don't feel strong. I am contented in hiding in my own fears. Thank God this is a fleeting thing and He comes to rescue me each time. Some times it takes longer than others to completely blow apart the barriers I surround myself with. But each time He brings me to a new awareness and level and fills in the holes with His love.

Michelle Elizabeth Rogers

HOW HE LOVES ME

Sometimes I am amazed how He can love me
For all of my sin, He did see.
There were times when I did not care,
Did what I wanted like He was not there.
And how regretful I am for all that was done
All the wickedness I disguised as harmless fun.
When I look back my eyes fill with tears,
Thinking back to all those wasted years.
Be He waited for me, blessing me everyday
Shinning His light upon my weary mane.
He lifted the fog so now I can truly see
All the blessings in my life and how He loves me.
He opened my heart and shined in His light
Cleaning out the corners as dark as night.
I asked Him in because I heard Him knock
I gave Jesus the only key and He threw away the lock.
He unlocked my heart and helped it to grow
Showing me more love than I have ever known.
I received Him as my Savior and gave Him my heart
Gave Him my soul, love and life; that was just a start.
Regretful and sorrowful of all my wicked ways
Repenting of them faithfully, each day.
For all of my sin, I asked Jesus to forgive
Asking Him to lead me and teach me how to live.
I am so thankful He lets me walk by His side,
To the narrow path I will follow, for He is my guide.
Grateful to accept the blessings that are free
And so very thankful of How He Loves Me.

John 10:9-11

I am the gate; whoever enters through me will be saved. He will come in and go out, and find pasture. The thief comes only to steal and kill and destroy; I have come that they may have life, and have it to the full. "I am the good shepherd. The good Shepherd lays down his life for the sheep."

My words,

I have trouble trusting people. Maybe because of something in my past or maybe because of all those times I have been let down and betrayed. There are only a few people now that I trust and those that I do, I cherish deeply. Because if I trust them, then I have given them my heart. It is the same with Jesus; I trust Him and gave Him my heart. Not saying that I trust Him completely all the time, I try to trust Him better with all things in my life. He knows all things about me, even the secrets and dark places in me and still He loves me.

Michelle Elizabeth Rogers

JESUS IS THE ONLY ONE

Others will tempt, others will lure
The world will promise to give so much more
But remember Jesus is the only Door.

It doesn't matter what you do or what you say
There is no where to buy it, no money can pay
Because Jesus is the only Way.

Darkness doesn't only come at night
Worldly pleasures will taint your sight
But don't let it take away what is right
That Jesus is the only Light.

Don't let the world infect your morals or couth
Don't let the world pull you from your spiritual roots
Remember that Jesus is the only Truth.

Don't fall into self-centered pleasing
The Spirit should last longer than the season
Because Jesus is the true Reason.

He is our Holy Father's Son
He has loved us since our life begun
And through His Blood our victory is won
Because Jesus is the only One.

John 11:25-26

Jesus told her, "I am the resurrection and the life. Those who believe in me, even though they die like everyone else, will live again. They are given eternal life for believing in me and will never perish. .

John 12:46

"I have come as a light to shine in this dark world, so that all who put their trust in me will no longer remain in the darkness."

John 14:6

Jesus said, "I am the way, the truth and the life, no one can come to the Father except through me."

My words,

It is all about Jesus! He is my hope, my faith, my rock, my light, my truth, my life and my salvation. It is described in the Bible as two paths; one is a narrow path to Heaven and a wide highway to destruction. The narrow path can sometimes be hard to travel, that is why Jesus is my everything. There is no other way I could travel that path! It is Jesus' way or the highway!

Michelle Elizabeth Rogers

Your Glory overwhelms me with Love...

Gently Wooing Me...

WHAT MAKES GOD SMILE

Is it laughter of the children, those pure at heart
Sweet little faces, with no care from the start?
They smile, they run, they play,
Such little angels, making God's day.
Could it be churches that praise is Holy Name
Singing to Heaven about His Glorious Reign?
Nothing could be better then to hear His people pray
As God listens to them all, each and every day.
It might be the goodness still left in this world,
The helping hands given by boys and girls.
Of the hope that still lingers upon this land
And the people who are wise not to build on the sand.
Maybe it is the love that shines in every soul
With faith and trust God has made us whole.
He is true love that is plain to see,
There is nothing greater than Him loving me.
What makes God smile is all that He can see
In each heart and soul of those truly free.
He knows His children and He loves us all
Even those who do not know, even those who fall.

Proverbs 15:3

The eyes of the Lord are in every place, beholding the evil and the good.

Job 37:14

Stop and consider God's wonders.

My words,

There are times I wonder why God still keeps the world around. So much violence, destruction and filth in this world. But then I see the wonders of this world; kindness and love, sometimes few and far between, but it is still there. His Glory shown in nature. I love big birds, eagles, hawks, owls, and falcons. They mesmerize me so high in sky gliding so freely on the air. I was visiting my grandmother in Florida, I just started to take my dog for a walk when a heard a squawk over my head. I looked up and saw one of the most beautiful sights I had ever seen. A brown hawk flew about 6 inches over my head. Its beautiful wings were spread as it glided on the air, I turned to watch it gain height as it flapped its powerful wings. God's beauty was given as a gift for me. Euphoria for my eyes and spirit!

Michelle Elizabeth Rogers

UP ABOVE THE CLOUDS

On days like this, I sit and I dream
The clouds have rolled in; gray and dreary it seems.
But then I sprout winds and I can fly
Up into the clouds, flying so high.
It only takes a minute, and then I break through the mist
Then God welcomes me to this place with a kiss.
I can't see the ground, looking like marshmallows at my feet
Purple and orange, blue and red, the colors gently meet.
The sky is deepest blue, not a cloud in sight
They all lay at my feet, so billowy and white.
The sun is so brilliant, glowing yellow and gold
It warms me through my flesh and my skin is no longer cold.
I can run through the puffs like a child at play
Or look up at the sky and wonder as I rest and lay.
But as the sun begins to retire, and fall out of my sight
The moon then appears and so it is night.
Billions of stars then begin to shine
Hanging so close, almost like they were mine.
They were placed out there by God, calling them all by name
Just like snowflakes, not one is the same.
Their light is bright, casting shadows upon the clouds
And I feel so blessed to be standing here above the crowds.
For I am standing in the presence of God's beautiful Face
And I see His fingerprints on every part of this place.
So when it is dark and dreary all around
Up above the clouds is where I will be found.

Psalm 19:1-5

The heavens declare the glory of God; the skies proclaim the work of his hands. Day after day they pour forth speech; night after night they display knowledge. There is no speech or language where their voice is not heard. Their voice goes out into all the earth, their words to the ends of the world. In the heavens he has pitched a tent for the sun, which is like a bridegroom coming forth from his pavilion, like a champion rejoicing to run his course.

My words,

I don't mind the rain, but when the clouds roll in and stay for days at a time, that is what I don't like. Certainly the sun hasn't gone on vacation, it is still there, but it sure doesn't feel like it. I try to imagine what it looks like above the clouds. So when I imagine, I can see myself there and what a magnificent sight it would be. What a gift imagination is, I don't know where I would be without it!

Michelle Elizabeth Rogers

THE DEW ON THE GRASS

I walk in the field and my feet are bare,
Here I can run and play without a worry, without a care.
The sun has just broke the horizon plane
And laid an overdue smile upon my weary mane.
My eyes have just opened for the first time today,
Hope was restored to help me walk along this hard way.
My feet are soaked and cold from the dew, but I don't mind
Because this time of the morning, I am alive.
With blessings from God showering down upon me
The sun is so bright, but it doesn't blind me, I can see.
The sky is so blue with ribbons of color cascading by
And a breeze catches under me and makes me fly.
My heart fills with love and I see His glory unfold
Not realizing He is wooing me, my heart He holds.
I love these early morning walks when my mind is this clear
Basking in His Glory, feeling His presence so near!
I can see for miles, no progress to invade my sight
And in His presence, my burdens are light.
I need this time each day when I awake
To stand in God's presence and my heart for Jesus to take.
And when the dew is on the grass each day,
I will walk in His presence along the way.

John 10:27-28

My sheep listen to my voice; I know them and they follow me. I give them eternal life, and they shall never perish; no one can snatch them out of my hand.

My words,

When I was a child, of course I was up at the crack of dawn. I loved to be barefoot and walk through the cool, wet grass. A time that is quiet of noise, but voluble with songs and sounds. Enjoying the freeness and just loving life. Just to be in His presence as I take in the wonders of His Glory. Early morning summer is still my favorite time and it still feels the same.

Michelle Elizabeth Rogers

AFTER THE SUN SETS

The sky begins to dim and its colors begin to change
It deepens with feeling, cascading its emotion like it turned the page.
The horizon opens up and swallows in the sky
Gently pulling the sun down from upon high.
After the sun sets the clouds turn gray
They lose their color from earlier in the day.
Now the stress and headaches begin to fade
As eyes watch the wonder God has made.
Birds add style as they fly through the mist
Touching the sky like a soft, sweet kiss.
The air turns cooler as the heat is drawn away
Now somewhere else it is turning into day.
As the blue darkens, the stars begin to appear
Trickled on the face on the sky like a tear.
Shadows come as the set begins to close
As do the troubles of the day and all of its woes.
After the sun sets calmness rolls in
All grows quiet as though it was sleeping.
Peace fills the air like a gentle white dove
A hope for tomorrow is given from God in Heaven above.
Now the sky grows dark and all the colors fade away
After the sun sets God will bring a new day.

Psalm 113:2-4

Let the name of the LORD be praised, both now and forevermore. From the rising of the sun to the place where it sets, the name of the LORD is to be praised. The LORD is exalted over all the nations, his glory above the heavens.

My words,

God woos us with the beauty of this world. It is not by mistake all the wonderful and awesome things I have daily to behold. He is the Father giving His children the best of everything. He is the Most High that courts His children through love. He is the Almighty that comforts and strengthens His children. He is the Holy Father who is my everything and makes it possible for me to love others to a higher level, because He has taken me to higher ground.

Michelle Elizabeth Rogers

WHEN HONEYSUCKLES ARE IN BLOOM

When honeysuckles are in bloom the dream takes me away
To a place where the meadows I see every day.
The cool breeze blowing through my long and dark hair
And a gentle sweet smell fills the air.
I can lay in the field and find peace in the sky,
No time here to watch, just the butterflies.
The light warms the ground, for my feet are bare,
I can run through this field, for there are no tares.
Joy and happiness follow me wherever I go
And love and fulfillment is all I now know.
A beautiful sound rings through my ears
And the comfort I feel here lifts away my fears.
The colors in the flowers fill my wandering sight,
The morning turns into day, but there is no night.
A sea of colors flow through the gentle, soft breeze
Carrying the rainbow up higher than the highest trees.
I am by myself here, but I am never alone
I have a friend beside me wherever I roam.
The dream has no ending, it carries on
Although the winter may seem so very long.
But when it is time, I know it will be coming soon
Only when the Honeysuckles are in Bloom.

Psalm 19:7-9

The law of the LORD is perfect, reviving the soul. The statutes of the LORD are trustworthy, making wise the simple. The precepts of the LORD are right, giving joy to the heart. The commands of the LORD are radiant, giving light to the eyes. The fear of the LORD is pure, enduring forever. The ordinances of the LORD are sure and altogether righteous.

My words,

Springtime, when God wakes up the earth. Everything is anew! Birds sing and fill the air with sweet melody. Flowers bloom and fill the senses with fragrance. An excitement that all living things share. Even everything in me begins to awaken and rejoice in the renewing of nature. A gift given for the eyes to see, ears to hear and nose to smell all the wonders of God's glory.

Michelle Elizabeth Rogers

THANK YOU GOD

Thank you God for this beautiful day
For the trees that provide the cool shade,
For the soft breeze that cools us from the sun
For the little critters that play and run!
Thank you God for the birds that sing
For all the lovely melodies they bring,
For the way they fly through the open sky
And for their beauty, soaring way up high!
Thank you God, for the rain that falls
For the water that makes the trees so tall,
For the flowers that bloom and the beauty there
And for the sweet smell they leave in the air!
Thank you God, for the rivers, oceans and streams
For the heavenly sounds that sends us to our dreams,
For a cool dip on those hot summer days
And for beauty it reflects from the sun setting rays!
Thank you God for the bright blue sky
For the white billowy clouds way up high,
For the colors so perfect and pure
And for the hope it brings for each day to endure!
Thank you God for this beautiful place
For Your fingerprints on everything, Your Glory, Your Grace,
For Your Presence that we can find in everything we see
Thank you God for Your Love that is free!

Psalm 30:11-12

You turned my wailing into dancing; you removed my sackcloth and clothed me with joy, that my heart may sing to you and not be silent. O LORD my God, I will give you thanks forever.

II Corinthians 9:15

Thank God for His Son, a gift too wonderful for words!

My words,

Sometimes I think the words "thank you", just does not seem to be big enough. I thank God in all things, asking for forgiveness when I complain. I am so very blessed, but as a human I still moan, groan and complain. It is so very important to show gratitude and to say "thank you". Have you ever given a gift to someone who doesn't say or show "thanks"? It is not a nice feeling and makes me feel unappreciated, like why should I bother. I don't want my Lord to think that I am not appreciative of all that He has given me. So I will continue to thank Him in words, in song and in deeds.

Thank you God for the blessings in my life and thank you most of all for the Gift of Your Son!

Michelle Elizabeth Rogers

It is not by my works, but only by His Grace...

Saved by Grace...

GOD'S GRACE

God's Grace is not only for the righteous and the wise
It is also given to the sinners; He hears their cries.
God's Grace can't be bought with good deeds done,
It is given through Jesus, who is His only Son.
For this is a gift that is free to all
All that needs to be done is in the name of Jesus, call.
God's love is unfailing and faithful, it is written in the Word
He wants to give His blessings to everyone in the world.
To be perfect is not a requirement, to be righteous..no
Even to those who felt unworthy, His Love will know.
The self-righteous hypocrites have no right to condemn
And there is no one in human flesh that is without sin.
So don't rely on what mere humans say
Because God's Grace is for everyone, every day.
And take lightly what the world may hold
Because through Jesus Christ, we can come to the Throne bold.
A heart of anyone that shows the image of Christ's face
Will surely be blessed with God's love and His Grace!

Isaiah 40:28-29

The Lord is the everlasting God, the Creator of the end of the earth. He will not grow tired or weary, and His understanding no one can fathom. He giveth power to the faint, and to them that have no might He increases strength.

Proverbs 10:12

Hatred stirs up dissension, but love covers over all wrongs.

My words,

There are so many hypocrites that I have come into contact with. Even friends that I have known for years. In I Corinthians 4:3-4 it states: "I care very little if I am judged by you or by any human court; indeed, I do not even judge myself. My conscience is clear, but that does not make me innocent. It is the Lord who judges me."

My love is deep and my heart is free, I am in my Father and He is in me. Would He spend so much time molding me if I were unworthy? He has a plan for me and He sets the time for what sins from which He wants me to repent. The Bible states "love covers a multitude of sins". So I don't care what the hypocrites say because my relationship with Jesus is none of their business.

Michelle Elizabeth Rogers

MICHELLE ELIZABETH ROGERS

ON HOLY GROUND

I walk on Holy Ground, because He walks with me
I can feel His hand on my back guiding me.
The path is long and the hills are steep
But when we reach the top, He renews my feet.
He is strong, for His arms carry me when I am weak
And when I am tired, He watches over me while I sleep.
His love fills my heart as He calls me by name,
He comforts me in sorrow and takes away my pain.
I stand on Holy Ground, because He is standing there too,
Restoring my soul and making my heart new.
I am safe here; this ground will never shake
And there will never be a temptation too much to take.
I tell Him about everything as we walk along this way
For He is always walking beside me, night or day.
He is my rope if I should hit a wall
And when the path is too narrow, behind me He walks in case I fall.
We have traveled for miles and still many miles to go
But when the path becomes a tightrope, this I know,
He will be my balance stick, and I will make it fine
Or even if the path becomes the thinnest of lines.
For all along the straight and narrow He is found
And In His Presence we walk on Holy Ground!

Exodus 3:5

God said, "Take off your sandals, for the place where you are standing is holy ground.

My words,

God is everywhere and everywhere is holy ground. I will always try to walk with care and purpose, that all steps are directed by the Father in Heaven.

Michelle Elizabeth Rogers

HIS PRESENCE

I can't see Him with my eyes, but I know He is there,
I can't feel His fingers on my skin, but I know He cares.
His presence is all around in and outside of me,
He is my oxygen when I can't breathe.
He is my strength when I am weak
And if I should fall, He pulls me to my feet.
I bow in His presence when I praise Him on high,
I hide myself in Him when I am sad and need to cry.
He lives in my heart; He occupies my soul,
He keeps me warm when the world is so cold.
He led me on a path and carried me most of the way
And now He walks with me each day.
His presence shadows me when I am enslaved by fear
And the sweet song of The Holy Word opens mine ears.
He gives me His shoulder when I am filled with sorrow
Filling me with hope so I can face tomorrow.
His presence fills my eyes like a gentle mist of rain
And erases my suffering when I am in pain.
I put on His armor and it gives me strength to fight
Against the attacks of evil either day or night.
I am in His presence and His presence is in me
Engulfing my soul with His spirit and setting me free.
So now I can say that I am on the right side of the fence
Because I will forever live in His Presence.

Psalm 27:1

The Lord is my light and my salvation; whom shall I fear?
The Lord is the strength of my life; of whom shall I be afraid?

Psalm 91: 1

He who dwells in the shelter of the Most High will rest in the shadow of
the Almighty.

My words,

He is the air that I breathe; He is all the good in me. When I get caught
up in the hustle and bustle of this life I can feel distracted, apart and foggy. His
Presence is there always with me whether I can feel it or not. His Presence sur-
rounds me, side to side, top to bottom; always protecting me. So when I'm feeling
lost or afraid it is because I have let the world in too much. It is said in the Bible
that we are in the world, but should not be of the world. It can be hard at times;
I just need to remember when I feel it creep up, to get back in check.

Michelle Elizabeth Rogers

PERFECT CLEANSING

A perfect heart and pure blood was the final atonement
Given to all that believe and willing to repent.
He hung on a tree when God put all sin upon His chest
With suffering and pain, He died a shameful death.
I believe that this is why He saved me,
Cleansed me with His blood so eternity I would see.
Now my eyes are different, I can see His perfect will
And my ears are opened for His word now to fill.
I know now I can't do it on my own,
Trusting in Him is the best feeling I have ever known.
When I pray for my anger, worries, fears or pain,
One by one He takes them and I become sustained.
His Blood covered me like a waterfall of fire
Purifying my soul and taking it so much higher.
It soaked into ever crack, His Blood flows through me
And every dark corner was given light to set me free.
I have received His Perfect Cleansing, wanting now to keep it clean,
It is not easy, for I am still just a sinful human being.
But I know with a prayer and the words "forgive me", I can start again
Renouncing my old self, trying not to bend.
For He has given me His Grace and the Glory of His Blood
And I have found Perfect Cleansing underneath that powerful flood!

I Peter 1:18-20

For you know that it was not with perishable things such as silver or gold that you were redeemed from the empty way of life handed down to you from your forefathers, but with the precious blood of Christ, a lamb without blemish or defect. He was chosen before the creation of the world, but was revealed in these last times for your sake.

My words,

Like I said before, it is all about Jesus! The entire Old Testament prophesies about the coming of the Messiah. Thank you God that it was fulfilled and my Savior lives! Just one drop of His precious blood cleansed me of all my sins and will continue to cleanse each minute of each hour of each day! I am so thankful that I have been wanted and plunged underneath the cleansing flood.

Michelle Elizabeth Rogers

FIXED ON JESUS

Why are my eyes so fixed on the ground?
Because there, my life's purpose isn't found,
But still I watch where it is I walk
And rely on my own voice when I talk,
I live by the example set forth by man
Always looking for help from the wrong hand,
A change in mindset is what I need to begin,
To take the world away that is deep within.
Tilt my head back and open my eyes
Get my eyes fixed on Heaven way up high.
No longer listen to the world's clatter in my ears
And rely on Jesus to sustain my fears.
No need to watch where I now walk
Because it is His voice I will listen before I talk.
I don't want this world anymore, please take it away
I pray that He guides me and shows me His true way.
When trouble and temptation try to pull me down
It is through Jesus that my strength is found.
I no longer want part in this world's filth and decay,
I want my eyes fixed on Jesus so I won't lose my way.

Matthew 11:28-30

"Come to me, all you who are weary and burdened, and I will give you rest. Take my yoke upon you and learn from me, for I am gentle and humble in heart, and you will find rest for your souls. For my yoke is easy and my burden is light."

My words,

In the book of Matthew, it tells of Jesus walking on the water. When the disciples saw Him coming they were afraid, but Jesus called out to let them know it was He. Peter asked to walk on the water with Him. As Peter was walking with Him, he became afraid and started to sink in the water. Jesus pulled him up and asked, "Why did you doubt?" It is the same for whatever problem that I face, I am walking with Him, but as soon as I doubt I begin to sink. Keeping my eyes fixed on Jesus will keep my feet on whatever comes along; knowing that He will see me through it. I'm not perfect at trusting Him, so I still sink down at times. But I will always yell out "Save me!" and He is just and faithful to pull me up on solid ground again. I will continue to learn how to magnify Jesus and not the problem.

Michelle Elizabeth Rogers

HOW DO I THANK GOD

How do I thank God for all that He has given me
For the times I was blind and He helped me to see.
The times I stumbled, He always caught my fall
And the times He has helped me rise above it all.
When I was weak and wanted to hide,
God came and stood by my side.
If my eyes would fill with tears
It wasn't so bad because I knew He was near.
He gave me hope that tomorrow would be a better day
And He held my hand all along the way.
When my days were dark and full of fear,
His ear was there, for my prayers He would hear.
He gave me strength to walk in this life
He gave me faith to handle life's strife.
He gave me wings so I would not fall
And He gave me love, to love it all.
So how do I thank God for all He has given to me,
My fragile voice says over again "Thank you God for setting me free!"

Colossians 2:6-8

So then, just as you received Christ Jesus as Lord, continue to live in him, rooted and built up in him, strengthened in the faith as you were taught, and overflowing with thankfulness. See to it that no one takes you captive through hollow and deceptive philosophy, which depends on human tradition and the basic principles of this world rather than on Christ.

My words,

Sometimes I feel like I can't possibly thank God enough for all that He has given me. I know that all I have has been given to me through the blessings of God. And I know that all my talents and knowledge are gifts from God. Not only did He give them to me, but He also continues to renew them all the time!

Michelle Elizabeth Rogers

47085